COPING

SOCIAL MEDIA ANXIETY

ROBIN BAUSER

ROSEN PUBLISHING

Published in 2023 by The Rosen Publishing Group, Inc.
2544 Clinton St, Buffalo, NY 14224

First Edition

Designer: Rachel Rising
Editor: Corona Brezina

Portions of this work were originally authored by Jackson Nieuwland and published as *Coping with Social Media Anxiety*. All new material this edition authored by Robin Bauser.

Cataloging-in-Publication Data

Names: Bauser, Robin
Title: Social media anxiety / Robin Bauser.
Description: New York : Rosen, 2023. | Series: Coping|
Includes bibliographic references, index and glossary.
Identifiers: ISBN 9781499473773 (pbk) | ISBN 9781499473780
(library bound) | ISBN 9781499473797 (ebook)
Subjects: LCSH: Anxiety--Juvenile literature. | Mental health
--Juvenile literature. | Social Media--Juvenile literature
Classification: LCC HQ799.2.M35 B38 2023 | DDC 302.23--dc23

Some of the images in this book illustrate individuals who are models. The depictions do not imply actual situations or events.

Manufactured in the United States of America

CPSIA Compliance Information: Batch #CSRYA23. For further information contact Rosen Publishing at 1-800-237-9932.

CONTENTS

CHAPTER 1

ANXIETY AND SOCIAL MEDIA

Have you checked any of your social media accounts today? If so, you've probably noticed who liked your stuff, who shared it, and how many followers you gained or lost. Social media provides an immediate connection to family, friends, and countless other social media users across the world. It serves as a means of staying informed and sharing news. People enjoy the connections provided by social media, but a fixation on social media can lead to users craving constant validation or losing track of time repeatedly checking for updates.

There are many aspects of the phenomenon called social media anxiety, which affects users who have trouble balancing social media use with the rest of their lives. It can lead to people feeling anxious, stressed, and overwhelmed. Maybe you tell yourself that you're going to step back from social media, only to find yourself back on your usual platforms the first moment that you're at loose ends. Social media is pervasive in our everyday lives, and it's hard to break a habit as a heavy user, even if you recognize that it's having unhealthy effects on your mental health.

SOCIAL MEDIA EVERYWHERE

Even if you don't use social media, you can't avoid it. There are tweets on the news, people posting Facebook statuses on the bus, and countless Snapchat messages to keep up with. You can probably name a half dozen social media platforms off the top of your head: Facebook, Twitter, Instagram, TikTok, Pinterest, Tumblr, LinkedIn. But actually defining social media is more difficult than you might think, especially because new social media platforms are launching all the time, each one potentially expanding the limits of how social media can be defined.

Many people use social media apps on their smartphones. Typically, about half of the top apps downloaded from the Apple App Store every week are related to social media.

Every social media platform has a different set of features, so how do we decide what it is that makes a website or an app a form of social media? Is YouTube social media? What about Reddit? In order to create a definition of social media, we need to determine what these platforms have in common: they are based online, you need an account to use them, you can use your account to connect with other users, and the content on the platform is generated by the users.

Each social media platform specializes in certain niches, such as video streaming or professional networking, and attracts a different audience.

So social media can be broadly defined as platforms that allow the sharing of user-generated content through profile-based online networks. Or more simply put: websites or apps where you can sign in and share things with your friends are forms of social media.

UNDERSTANDING ANXIETY

Anxiety is a feeling of worry, stress, or inner turmoil about a future event. Although this might seem similar to fear, there is an important difference between the two. Fear is triggered by an immediate, objective danger, whereas anxiety is based on anticipation. It comes from thinking about things that might happen or go wrong and is often more long-lasting than fear. For instance, you would feel fear if a car was speeding toward you with no sign of stopping, but you would feel anxious if you worried about being hit by a car every time you crossed the street.

Anxiety is not a mental disorder on its own, but it is a symptom of many mental disorders, and many mental disorders have the word "anxiety" in their names, such as social anxiety disorder and generalized anxiety disorder. In fact, according to the National Institute of Mental Health, usually 19.1 percent of adults experience anxiety disorders in a given year, making them the most common form of mental illness in the United States. Not only that, but the average age of onset for some anxiety disorders is before 15 years old, meaning that these disorders can continue for years, from childhood into adulthood.

Social media can contribute to anxiety and depression. A mental health professional can help you improve your relationship with social media.

Although the term "social media anxiety disorder" is used by some people to describe social media anxiety, this term was coined by Julie Spira, an online dating expert who does not have a degree in psychology, and it is not a recognized clinical condition. This is not to say that social media anxiety is not a serious issue or that it won't one day be classified as a mental disorder. It is still a developing area of study, and you need to make sure you're getting your information from credible sources. If you think you are suffering from an anxiety disorder, you should seek the opinion of a qualified medical professional.

So how do networks designed to help you keep in touch with your friends cause so much turmoil that people are coming up with medical terms for the phenomenon? The answer varies from one person to another. No one's experience is exactly the same as anyone else's, but there are three main factors that contribute to social media anxiety: fear of missing out, overstimulation, and low self-esteem. In some cases, social media magnifies a preexisting problem. In others, it triggers something that hadn't existed previously.

DO YOU HAVE FOMO?

"Fear of missing out" (FOMO) is a term born on the internet, and while it doesn't only apply to social media it does contribute significantly to social media anxiety. Social media has become one of the main ways people keep up to date with the world around them. Not only can it be used to stay in touch with friends, but it is also a news source, a way to plan and invite people to events, a place to search for jobs and accommodation, and much more. Users of social media often feel a need to keep checking their feeds in order to make sure they don't miss anything important, and when they don't have access to social media, they sometimes feel anxious that there might be something happening on social media that they should be seeing.

The problem is that it is physically impossible to keep up with everything that happens online—there's just too much of it—and so it's also impossible not to be missing out on something. FOMO leads people to use social media more and more often to avoid missing out. This of course causes more problems.

Social media is so extensive that you can feel anxious that you're missing out on something on social media even when you're on social media.

Not only do people worry about missing out on things that happen on social media, but when they're on social media, they worry about missing out on the events their friends are posting about attending. When they see photos of their friends going to the movies together, they wonder why they weren't invited and what else they've been left out of. If this happens to you, try to remember that you weren't intentionally excluded.

INFORMATION OVERLOAD

When we sign into our social media accounts, we are bombarded with information. And people aren't even looking at just one social media platform at a time. Tabbed browsing allows people to quickly click between multiple websites. In less than a minute, someone could go from scrolling through Instagram to filming a Snapchat to checking Facebook notifications. This is more than the human brain is designed to cope with.

There's so much content on social media that it's easy to lose track of time checking updates on various platforms.

When people are browsing social media on their phones or computers, they are often doing something else at the same time, whether it's listening to music, watching television, writing an essay, or having a conversation. This is called multitasking. Unfortunately, humans aren't wired to multitask. What people are actually doing in these situations is switching back and forth between tasks very quickly, and this takes a toll.

Trying to juggle these different tasks actually changes people's brain chemistry. So-called multitasking causes increased levels of cortisol (the stress hormone) and adrenaline (the fight-or-flight hormone), which can overstimulate the brain, causing erratic thoughts. It's the perfect recipe for anxiety.

Focusing on a single activity is more efficient than multitasking—people have to refocus their attention whenever they switch from one task to another, making errors more likely.

SELF-ESTEEM AND SOCIAL MEDIA

Low self-esteem was a problem long before the invention of social media and it will continue to be a problem even if we stop using social media altogether. But for people with low self-esteem, social media can be an extremely damaging place. It can also lead to low self-esteem in people who were previously very confident in themselves.

The connection between social media and low self-esteem is rooted in the way people compare themselves to others online. Social media provides users with more access than ever before to other peoples' lives. They see their friends hanging out without them, cooking delicious meals, and falling in love. They see their workmates going on exotic holidays, buying new cars, and celebrating promotions. They see celebrities going to the gym, wearing expensive clothing, and attending exclusive events. People inevitably compare themselves to the posts they see online. What they don't always realize is that this isn't a fair comparison.

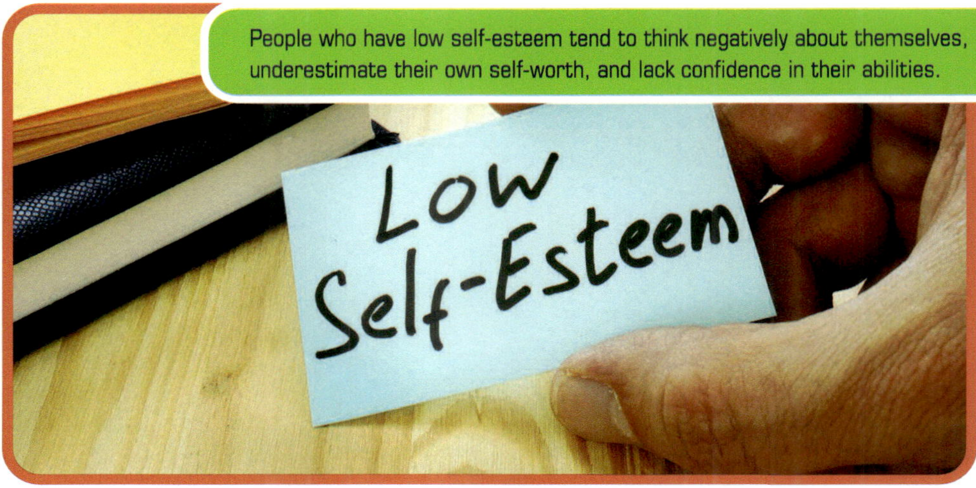

People who have low self-esteem tend to think negatively about themselves, underestimate their own self-worth, and lack confidence in their abilities.

People curate, or carefully manage, their social media presences as a way to present the best possible version of themselves. Most of the time, they only share things online that they think are impressive or funny. So, when people compare themselves to their friends on social media, they are judging themselves against an impossible standard, because they are comparing themselves in their current state to their friends at their very best. When you're feeling bad about not measuring up to what your friends are posting online, remember this: they could be trying to make themselves look good because they're insecure, too. They probably feel like they don't measure up to what you're posting yourself.

One reason people only post the most flattering content on social media is that they want to make themselves look better than they think they are.

This cycle of low self-esteem is fueled by the design of these platforms. Most social media platforms have a "like" or "favorite" feature. People judge the value of their posts (and therefore themselves) on how many likes they receive. This results in users basing their self-worth on external praise. It is an unreliable way to assess yourself, because you have no control over how many people like your posts. Sure, you feel good when one of your selfies gets a lot of likes, but that feeling doesn't last. If your next post doesn't get the same response, you could be plunged into self-doubt.

There are many causes of anxiety, but one of the sources in people's everyday lives is stress. Stress can result from serious emotional trauma as well as smaller issues or setbacks that can add up over time. These three factors combined—FOMO, overstimulation, and low self-esteem—create a situation that can easily become stressful, especially if you can't force yourself to stay away from social media. This stress can contribute to a sense of anxiety triggered by social media interactions.

MYTHS & FACTS

MYTH: Things that happen online don't matter because they're not "real."

FACT: There are plenty of things that happen online that have real effects on people's lives. Just because someone says something to you online, rather than in person, doesn't mean it has any less effect on you. To suggest that cyberbullying, long-distance relationships, and online classes aren't "real" is inaccurate. These events influence people's lives just as much as the things that happen to them offline.

MYTH: People who post a lot of selfies are vain.

FACT: A 2016 study by Yongjun Sung found four core reasons why people post selfies online: attention seeking, communication, archiving, and entertainment. Of those four reasons, only attention seeking is sometimes linked to vanity. Plenty of people are sharing their selfies on social media because they find it fun or to document that they were doing something at a certain time. Also, the people who are posting selfies to get attention are often not doing so to show off but are actually trying to gain the validation or approval of their friends or peers.

MYTH: Social media is a waste of time.

FACT: Although this resource is focused on one of the negative effects of social media, that doesn't mean that it doesn't have any positives. For many people, social media is both enjoyable and fulfilling. Users rely on social media to keep in touch with friends and family and foster connections with people from different regions, countries, and cultures. It's a valuable source of local news and opportunities, from housing to community events to educational resources. People use social media for career networking, to raise awareness for charities, and to organize movements for positive social change.

Social media plays a key role in people's daily lives, serving as a source of social connections, entertainment, news updates, and professional opportunities.

CHAPTER 2

RECOGNIZING SOCIAL MEDIA ANXIETY

If you're a social media user, you might be wondering whether you suffer from social media anxiety, especially if you have a general tendency to feel anxious. But most teens use social media, and there are many types of anxiety disorders. Social media isn't necessarily the root cause of your anxiety.

Social media anxiety isn't a clinical condition recognized by mental health professionals. There's no standardized definition, and not everybody with social media anxiety experiences all of the same symptoms. But if you've observed that your feelings of anxiety are closely linked to your social media use, it's an indication that you may have social media anxiety. Here are some of the symptoms and behaviors linked to social media anxiety.

FOCUSING ON THE PRESENT

Often, people experiencing social media anxiety feel anxious when they are unable to check social media. This feeling of anxiety can make it difficult to focus on other tasks. It's hard to write an essay when you're busy wondering how many likes the latest photo you shared on Instagram has gotten. And that's assuming you have the discipline not to check social media while you're writing the essay.

Modern society places a high value on multitasking. The only problem is that we can't actually perform several tasks at once effectively, and it's not just because it's hard to focus on two or more things at the same time.

Multitasking creates what the neuroscientist Daniel J. Levitin calls a "dopamine-addiction feedback loop," in which the brain is actually rewarded for losing focus and searching for something new to pay attention to. This happens because multitasking is not actually doing multiple things at once but rather switching between different tasks very quickly. Whenever people switch to a new task, the brain's prefrontal cortex releases a burst of endogenous opioids (brain chemicals that make you feel good), which basically rewards them for straying from the task at hand. It's easy to tell yourself you'll just quickly check your notifications and get a quick blast of dopamine before continuing with your work, but it's hard to focus when your brain is literally working against you.

Even if you do manage to avoid the dangers of multitasking, the mere opportunity to check social media actually decreases your ability to focus. A study by the psychiatrist Glenn Wilson found that when you are trying to focus on a task but are aware that there is an unread email waiting in your inbox, your IQ can be reduced by up to 10 points.

TROUBLE SLEEPING

Social media doesn't just cause sleep loss because people keep browsing late into the night (although this is a problem for some people). Social media causes insomnia through the effect it has on people's brains. The act of staring at a bright screen and concentrating on social media actually delays the brain's ability to get to sleep. This is because the screens of computers and phones emit a lot of blue light. Blue light signals to the brain that it is morning and time to wake up. The blue light suppresses melatonin, the hormone that regulates sleep. Usually, people's melatonin levels rise right before bedtime, but this suppression results in people struggling to get to sleep, and even when they do get to sleep, they are less likely to reach REM sleep (the most restorative phase of the sleep cycle). If our screens emitted red light, however, they would actually help us get to sleep, because red light signals to the brain that it is evening.

Not only does social media affect our brain chemistry, but it also has major effects on people's social expectations. Because of social media, people are now expected to be available 24 hours a day. Giving in to this pressure to be accessible means getting less sleep, but so does the stress of not giving into it.

Even once you've gotten to sleep, you're not safe. Many people sleep with their phones within reach, especially if they use their phones as alarm clocks. Unfortunately, sometimes your phone can wake you earlier than you had planned. More and more often, people are being woken in the night by notifications from social media, the light and buzzing from their phones disturbing their sleep. Also, when people wake up during the night, there is the danger of them checking social media. Then they again run the risk of blue light tricking their brain into thinking that it's morning. It's a cycle of sleeplessness that's not doing anyone any favors.

It can be hard to fall asleep when you're lying in bed just picturing the posts and messages piling up that will have to be dealt with next time you sign in.

SOCIAL MEDIA OBSESSION

Yes, it seems obvious, but checking social media an unreasonable amount can be one of the most obvious ways to realize that someone has a problem with social media. Although there are other possible causes for insomnia or for having trouble focusing, if you find yourself checking out TikTok when someone is in the middle of telling you exciting news, it's pretty clear TikTok has something to do with your lack of focus.

This compulsive use of social media can have a range of negative effects on people's lives. It can distract people from everyday tasks, which can be as minor as folding laundry or as high risk as driving to school. It can also damage personal relationships. Though the primary use of social media is to connect with other people, if you're still checking it while in the same room as friends, they could easily take offense.

Prioritizing social media over other forms of communication can often mean valuing surface-level interactions over deeper connections. It's much easier to like someone's Facebook status than to actually have a conversation with him about what's going on in his life. Though you may think you know people you have connected with through social media, there are probably many things about them that they don't share online.

Social media amplifies these types of false connections. According to evolutionary psychologist Robin I. M. Dunbar, people have layers of friendship. The highest layer can hold only a couple of people, perhaps a partner and a best friend, whom you share more with than anyone else. The second layer can hold at most four people with whom you have strong relationships that require weekly upkeep. After that, the layers hold more casual friends. Spending hours every day interacting with dozens of people online can mislead you into thinking you have more close friends than you really do and take time away from your most important relationships.

It's easy to rack up hundreds or even thousands of "friends" without having to spend any time maintaining relationships with the people behind the profile pictures.

CHASING THE INFLUENCERS

The most popular accounts on some social media platforms don't necessarily belong to celebrities. Influencers are online personalities with sizable audiences who focus primarily on a certain niche, such as beauty, fitness, fashion, business, or lifestyle. Their followers enjoy their content and pay attention to their recommendations. As a result, many influencers publish brand-sponsored posts touting products and services. For some companies, partnering with social media influencers has become a standard component of their marketing strategies.

Many young people who grew up with social media can easily see themselves becoming influencers by monetizing, or making money from, their interests or area of expertise. Becoming an influencer requires creativity, ambition, entrepreneurial spirit, and clever self-promotion. Even micro-influencers with fewer than 100,000 followers can make solid earnings through sources such as sponsored posts, sales, and ads. But being an influencer isn't always the dream that people imagine. Influencers can be subject to criticism and abuse. Their followers are often intolerant of any departure from the influencer's usual niche or persona. Influencers can have trouble disengaging from social media, resulting in anxiety and decreased self-confidence.

Influencers command a sizable online audience, and companies view them as a means of reaching potential customers through paid influencer endorsements.

MAINTAINING A BALANCE

Most of the time, social media anxiety is characterized by feeling anxious while unable to check social media, but in some cases the reverse can be true. Some people with social media anxiety feel anxious about checking social media. They worry about the news and updates waiting for them on social media, and so they avoid signing in to their accounts even when they have important reasons to do so. Although these people may not spend as much time on social media as others with social media anxiety, they still spend an unhealthy amount of time thinking about it.

Avoiding social media can lead to people isolating themselves. For many people, social media is their main way of keeping in touch with friends and family. People who avoid social media can easily fall out of touch and lose important relationships. Not going on social media also deprives them of the ability to share what is happening in their own lives, which can represent the loss of an important support system. This is not only a social issue. People who avoid using social media can miss out on significant personal and professional opportunities because they aren't putting themselves in the right position to grasp them.

There's no one-size-fits-all solution to social media anxiety. Frequently, the main cause of the problem is overuse—social media takes up too big a part of your life. But the problem can also be your attitude towards social media or, as seen, a harmful avoidance of social media that doesn't address the real reasons that social media induces anxiety. Shunning social media can just mean that you're trading one set of problems for another. The solution is to find a balance in terms of both mindset and time management where you can maintain a healthy relationship with social media.

Some people may try to avoid social media because they have used it too much in the past and suffered from the negative effects of social media overuse.

CHAPTER 3

RESETTING YOUR RELATIONSHIP WITH SOCIAL MEDIA

If you want to conquer social media anxiety, you need to change your behavior when you engage with social media. This may mean spending less time on social media platforms overall, or it could mean adjusting your everyday social media habits. You may even manage to beat your social media anxiety simply by changing your own perspective toward social media.

In order to adjust your relationship with social media, you need to analyze your own patterns of use. How much time do you spend on social media sites every day? When and where do you tend to log on? How many platforms do you use regularly? Once you understand what aspect of your social media use is contributing to your anxiety, you can figure out how you can change your behavior to bring balance to your social media habits.

TIME SPENT ON SOCIAL MEDIA

The average American uses social media for over two hours a day, according to Statista. Common Sense Media claims that 13- to 18-year-olds spend about 1.5 hours a day on social media. Keep in mind that these are averages; some people don't use social media at all, and others use it even more than these figures suggest. If you're struggling with social media anxiety, it may be because you are spending too much time on social media and becoming dependent on it. Try recording how much time you spend on social media in one day

If you're unhappy with the amount of time you're spending on social media or you think it's contributing to your social media anxiety, it's time to try cutting back. The most effective way to cut down the amount of time you spend on social media each day is to set a strict limit—one hour, for example. You can break up this time in any way you choose: half an hour in the morning then another half hour in the evening, 12 five-minute bursts throughout the day, or one long session. The only rule is that once your time is up, it's up.

If you're finding this too difficult, you may be trying too much all at once. It can be very difficult to break habits and change routines. Perhaps try setting a higher, more achievable limit. If you've had some success holding yourself to four hours of social media a day, you can cut out half hour segments until you reach a point where you feel good about the amount of time you're spending on social media. Once you've achieved this, all you have to do is maintain it.

All those quick glances at Twitter on your tablet add up. You might be surprised by how much of your day is taken up scrolling through your feeds.

Don't get too down on yourself if you do occasionally slip up and go over your social media limit. If something especially important or exciting happens one day, maybe it's OK to spend longer than usual on social media talking to people about it. Occasionally spending extra time on social media isn't going to do you any harm. The important thing here is managing habits: if you find yourself overusing social media on a more regular basis, it may be time to think of other ways to control your usage.

An important thing to steer away from is using social media right before bed because of the effect it can have on your sleep, but even this doesn't affect everyone. Some people sleep just fine after looking at Instagram for a few hours. It's all about figuring out your relationship with social media. After some experimenting, hopefully you'll be able to find certain times of day (or even days of the week) when using social media doesn't have such a negative effect on your mental well-being. Try to confine your social media use to those times: it could have a huge effect on your anxiety levels.

Too much social media around bedtime can affect your sleep—you're likelier to go to bed later and have more trouble falling asleep.

YOUR SOCIAL MEDIA ZONES

Much like when you use social media, where you use social media can have an impact on whether it causes you anxiety. Often, where you use social media is related to what else you are doing, or meant to be doing, while you're spending time networking. If you spend a lot of time on LinkedIn at work, then you're probably not getting much of your actual work done, which can lead to worry about deadlines and fear of being caught while off task. As a way of dealing with that stress and further avoiding your work, you may end up spending even more time on LinkedIn, creating a cycle of social media anxiety.

One way to combat social media anxiety is to set up social media–free zones, places where you're not allowed to use social media. If you often find yourself checking Facebook during dinner while the rest of your family is talking about their days, that might have a negative effect on your relationship with them. Other places to consider making social media off-limits are school, work, your bedroom, and social events. These are the places where social media is most likely to have a negative effect on your well-being, but, of course, it's different for everyone. You need to figure out where social media works for you.

You could even consider making your phone or tablet itself a social media–free zone by deleting all of your social media apps. This would mean you could only use social media when actually in front of a computer, which would significantly decrease the amount of multitasking involved. It would also further limit when you could use social media. It might take some time to get used to, but this type of controlled environment could be extremely useful for combating anxiety.

Once you get accustomed to only using social media in certain places at certain times, you will learn not to spend energy worrying about it the rest of the time.

CHOOSING YOUR PLATFORMS

Another part of your relationship with social media to consider is how many and which different platforms you're using. Maybe the reason you're spending too much time online is that you're trying to keep up with more platforms than you can manage. Perhaps you only find one or two of those platforms satisfying and the others are just adding stress to your life. If that's the case, it's probably time to cut down on the number of platforms you're using.

Every social media platform has a different focus and design. They all have their pros and cons. If your social media anxiety stems from not wanting to miss out on events your friends are attending, then you might want to stick with the app you use most with your friends and delete a couple of your other accounts. If your problem is that you're constantly sending Snapchats, then perhaps you should delete Snapchat from your device and try just using other social media platforms for a while.

According to statistics from Backlinko, the typical social media user actively uses 6.6 different platforms. If you're feeling overwhelmed by how much is happening on social media that you need to stay up-to-date with, you are probably using too many different platforms. Try to figure out which ones you get the most out of, keep those accounts, and delete the rest. There's no point in having an account on a social media platform if all it's doing is causing you anxiety.

Another thing to consider is how many people you are connected with on each platform. According to Statista, about 60 percent of Facebook users have over 200 Facebook friends. Professor Dunbar has found that the human brain cannot maintain relationships with many more than 150 people. So, if you're finding social media overwhelming, perhaps it's not because you're using too many platforms, but because you're connected with too many people on the platforms you do use. If you have a lot of friends on a particular social network, perhaps you should try unfollowing some of them and see how it affects your mental state.

Having a large number of connections on social media doesn't necessarily reflect a sense of personal connection with online friends or followers.

YOUR PERSONAL BRAND AND IMPOSTER SYNDROME

Some social media users intentionally set out to establish their own personal brand associated with their online presence. This is particularly true of career-oriented individuals. Companies research prospective employees online, and a stellar online reputation can help you land jobs. Your personal brand conveys who you are and how your strengths make you stand out from everyone else. It allows opportunities for networking, establishing authority in a certain niche, and reaching a wider audience.

The flip side of personal branding is imposter syndrome—self-doubt that prevents a person from truly believing they're worthy of the reputation and respect they've attained through their accomplishments. Someone with imposter syndrome fears that they're a fraud despite being seen as a success. Social media can intensify imposter syndrome. People instinctively compare themselves to the curated and seemingly ideal lives of other social media users and feel that they come up short. If social media makes you feel inadequate, remember that many of the people you're comparing yourself to probably feel the same way.

Imposter syndrome and social media anxiety are both linked to low self-esteem, which can be made worse by comparisons to other people's social media posts.

TOOLS TO CURB SOCIAL MEDIA

Social media is a tool that people use to keep in touch with friends and family, connect with new people who share similar interests, share their creative work, and record significant memories. All of this is positive and should be encouraged. It's when we become too dependent on it that the tool of social media stops being a benefit and starts causing us problems. But there are some other tools that can help us control our relationship with social media so that we can enjoy the benefits without the negative effects.

Using your phone's alarm clock function might be convenient, but it can also tempt you to log in to social media.

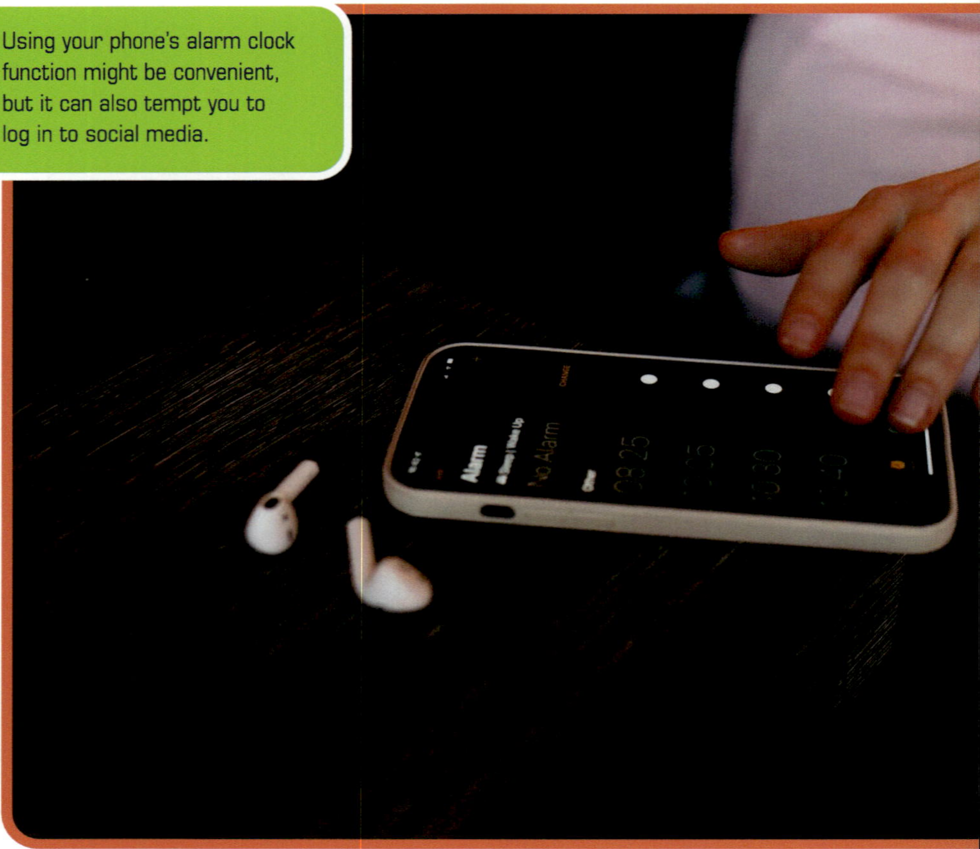

One thing that can really help is investing in an alarm clock. If the first thing you do when you wake up is pick up your phone to turn the alarm off, it can be tempting to check social media right away instead of getting up and getting ready for the day. Having an alarm clock also means that you don't have to keep your phone within arm's reach all night long (you could even keep it in another room), so you won't be disturbed by notifications during the night.

There is a whole range of apps out there specifically designed to help you track and control how much time you spend on social media. Apps like Offtime and Breakfree have many functions, like providing analysis of how you use your phone, monitoring your goals of how much you want to use your phone, blocking the use of certain apps for certain periods of time, auto-rejecting phone calls—the list goes on and on. If you're struggling to manage your social media use on your own, these apps can be very helpful. Trying to maintain a low "addiction score" can even become a kind of game.

Your phone itself probably has a few features that can help you manage your social media use. All smartphones have a built-in option called Flight Mode, which prevents your phone from sending or receiving signals. If you need to get some homework done without distractions, it might help to put your phone on airplane mode. Many phones also have other means of limiting their use, often designed to prevent children from accessing inappropriate content, but usually just as useful for controlling your social media use. For example, iPhones have a section in their settings called Restrictions, which allows you to block your phone from using specific apps or visiting particular websites. And there's always the last resort: the trusty power button. Sometimes the best solution is the simplest, and it makes the most sense just to turn your phone off.

You might learn a lot about yourself as you try to cut back on your social media use. People may find that reaching for their phone and checking social media is so automatic that they never realized how frequently they do it. When they manage to curb the impulse, some people report feeling more productive and creative, and they gain a sense of control. If your realignment of your relationship with social media is effective, keep up the good work. Try reassessing your social media use periodically to ensure that you maintain a healthy balance. But if small adjustments haven't managed to alleviate your social media anxiety, you might try more drastic measures.

A resolution to cut back on social media dependence can serve as an opportunity for fostering in-person relationships with friends.

CHAPTER 4

TAKING A BREAK

Unplugging might sound like an extreme course of action, but it can improve your relationship with social media. Maybe you've become more sensitive to negativity on some platforms, or overwhelmed by the stream of your online friends' photos that leave you feeling worse about yourself. Stepping back can help clarify which aspects of social media you find valuable and which cause you anxiety.

Plan ahead if you're going to unplug from social media. Decide how long you're going to be away, and let people know beforehand. Set some goals that you aim to accomplish during your time away from social media.

SETTING A TIMETABLE

Once you've decided to unplug, the next decision you need to make is how long you're committing to do it for. If you don't set an end date for your social media fasting, you are much more likely to give up early. There's no right or wrong length of time to give up social media. If you just want to see what it's like and what your immediate reaction to it is, you could sign out for just 24 hours. Or, if you're committed to making a significant change to your lifestyle, you could try a week or even a month.

For whatever period of time you decide to unplug, it's important to make sure that your goal is realistic and that you are prepared for everything it entails. It's probably not a good idea to decide today that you want to unplug for a year and then deactivate all your accounts right away.

You don't want to delete all your social media accounts and then realize that you have no way of contacting your best friend.

If you're planning to unplug for an extended period of time, you will want to check that you have other ways to get in touch with the important people in your life. Because there can be unexpected consequences to unplugging from social media, it is recommended that you start by unplugging for a short time first, say a week, and then building up to longer periods without social media. After all, if you reach the end of the time you had planned to unplug for and you want to keep going, there's no reason why you can't. Just set a new date you want to be social media–free until and see how you feel once you reach it.

NOTIFYING YOUR FRIENDS

Before you lock yourself out of social media, make sure you let people know what's about to happen. If you suddenly stop posting online, with no warning or obvious reason, the people who interact with you on social media might worry about you. They would have no way of knowing that this was something you had planned and could think that you were unwell or in danger.

It's a good idea to make a post on each of your social media accounts well in advance of unplugging (at least a couple of days before) to let everyone know that you won't be on social media for the foreseeable future. You can also use this post to give people alternate ways of contacting you, such as by email or text. If you don't want to make this information accessible to all the people with whom you're connected, you could write something such as "private message me for my email address" and only respond to people who you want to stay in touch with.

The reason it's important to make these kinds of posts in advance of unplugging is that you want to give people a chance to actually see them. If you make a post and then immediately delete your account, not many people are going to see it and there wouldn't have been much of a point in making it at all. Also, if you're asking your friends to message you to get your contact information, you need to give them time to do that.

If you don't make the effort to inform your friends about what you're doing and ensure that you can contact each other through other means, you run the risk of isolating yourself.

ONLINE TORMENT

It might seem that the internet should provide a refuge from bullying—kids can't be subjected to physical torment or humiliation in front of classmates when they're online. But cyberbullying can occur at any time or place through a variety of digital devices and platforms. Cyberbullying may involve direct communication, such as harassment or threats. A cyberbully can also post personal information, photos, or videos, or impersonate the target online to embarrass them. Since so much information shared online is permanent, cyberbullying can cause long-lasting damage. There are laws against cyberbullying and recourses for a target of cyberbullying. It's a bad idea to engage the bully—trying to retaliate is likely to worsen the situation. Instead, report the cyberbullying to a family member, teacher, or counselor. If the cyberbullying is taking place on social media, report the abuse to the platform. Save evidence of the harassment, such as screenshots or texts. Protect your data and update your privacy settings. You can also avoid cyberbullies by creating social media identities that you share only with your family and friends.

With each new social media platform that launches, there are new means and opportunities for bullies to abuse victims online.

LOCKING YOURSELF OUT

The next step is to lock yourself out of social media. Just signing out of your accounts isn't enough. You want to make it as difficult as possible for you to access your accounts, so you'll be less tempted to give up on your goal. You don't want it to be easy to sign back in and check social media without even thinking about it.

There are various ways of locking yourself out of your social media accounts. Some social media platforms make a distinction between deleting and deactivating your account. For instance, if you deactivate your Facebook account all of your information is retained on the website, but it can't be accessed by anyone unless you reactivate your account. Whereas if you delete your account, all of your information is lost forever, and it is impossible to get your account back. Both options have their pros and cons. If you deactivate your account, it's much easier to transition back into using Facebook once you've finished your time without social media, but reactivating your account only requires you to sign back in to your account, so it's much easier to give in to the temptation and return to Facebook. If you delete your account, however, there's no temptation to sign back in, because it's impossible. The downside is that when you decide to go back to using social media, you'll have to create a whole new account from scratch. If you decide to delete your accounts, make sure you save any information you don't want to lose. If Instagram is the only place you have your photos archived, you might want to download them onto your computer before deleting your account.

Another option is to change the passwords on your social media accounts to something that you don't know and then log out so that you won't be able to sign back in. If you choose this option, you need to make sure you'll be able to access your password once you're ready to return to social media. There are a few ways to do this: you could write the password down somewhere you're sure it won't get

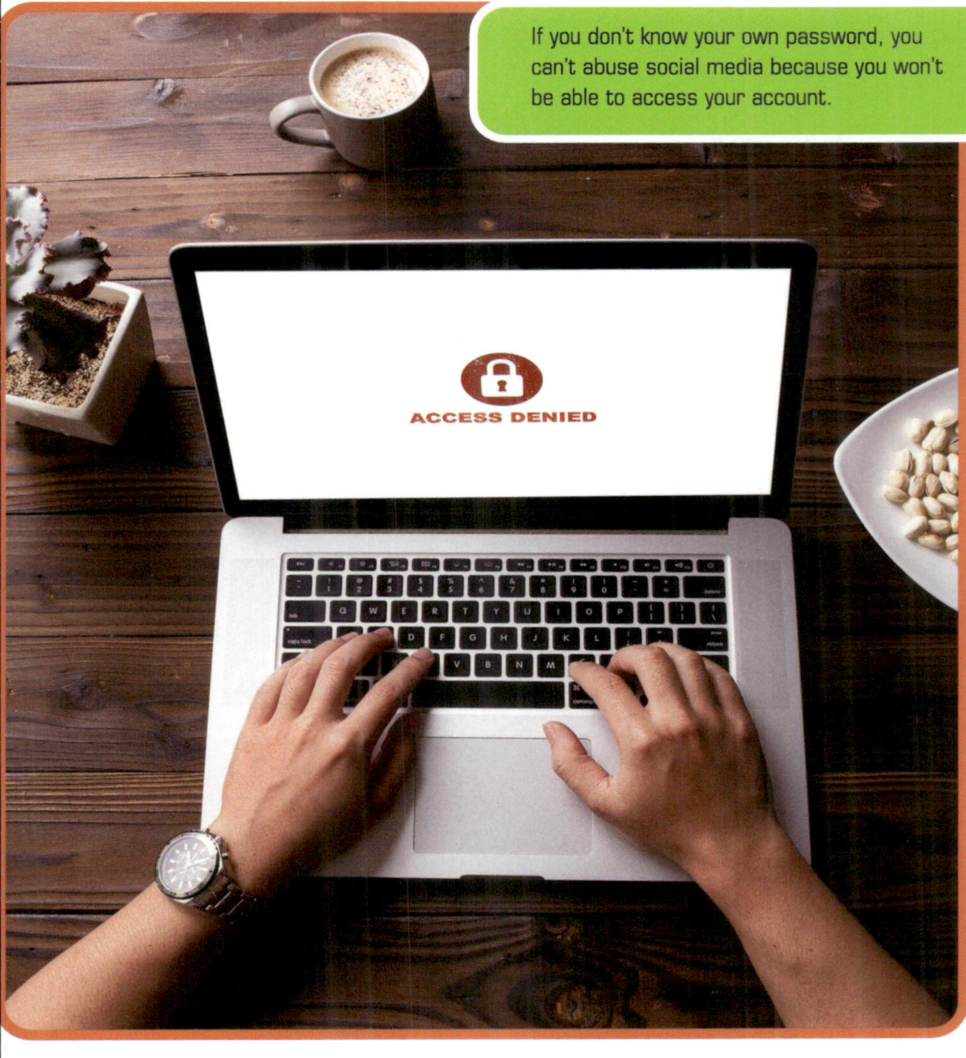

If you don't know your own password, you can't abuse social media because you won't be able to access your account.

lost, you could get a trusted family member to change the password for you, or you could just make sure that you know the answers to your security questions so you can use the "forgot your password" function. You've just got to make sure you don't give up and access your password before you've reached your goal.

Once you've locked yourself out, it's time to delete all the social media apps off your phone and/or tablet and block the websites on your computer. This will help by removing the constant reminders that you're avoiding social media, and it will lessen the temptation to give up and sign back in.

BEING SOCIAL AND KEEPING BUSY

It's important to make sure you don't isolate yourself during your time away from social media. It's increasingly common, especially among those with social media anxiety, for people to get the majority of their social interaction through social media. While you're unplugged, the key is to replace those interactions with other forms of communication.

There are plenty of ways to maintain a social life without using social media. You can call or text people, write letters or postcards, organize regular hangouts, meet friends for lunch or go to a movie together, or plan trips with people. During these interactions, you'll be spending more time with people than you

A positive aspect of in-person social activities is that they encourage more meaningful communication with people than you usually get from social media.

do when you quickly scan their status updates online. This extended and more focused time spent with people leads to stronger relationships with them. In addition to making sure you stay connected to your friends and family, time off of social media can also serve as an opportunity to connect with new people. It's not just social interactions that you will need to replace while you're off of social media. A lot of the time people spend on social media is not directly used to interact with their friends: much of it is spent aimlessly scrolling, checking to see if anything new has been posted even though they just looked two minutes ago, or clicking on links and reading articles that they never would have spent their time on if someone they knew hadn't shared it on social media.

It's important to find compelling things to fill the time you used to occupy with social media, because otherwise that time will be spent obsessing over the fact that you're not on social media, which isn't much of an improvement. This is a good chance to do some of the things you've always wanted to do but never had the time or discipline to follow through with: start exercising more, take an art class, or finally learn to knit. What kinds of activities you choose to use your new free time for can depend on how and when you used social media. If you always spent an hour first thing in the morning catching up on all your different feeds, then maybe you could use that time to go for a run or have a proper breakfast. Whereas, if you were a late-night Pinterest scroller, that time might be better spent writing in a journal or maybe even just getting to sleep earlier.

Another thing to consider is that many people habitually pull out their phones to check social media without even thinking about it or while they are waiting for something. It's useful to find something else to occupy yourself with in these situations, preferably something that involves

Taking a break from social media can offer opportunities to follow through on plans and goals that you've hoped to achieve.

using your hands, so it fills the same role as pulling out your phone. Maybe you could lose yourself in a book you've been planning to read.

As you finish your stint of unplugging, put some thought into how you want to ease yourself back into social media. According to a 2018 study, limiting social media time to 30 minutes daily improves users' overall sense of well-being. It might sound difficult, but recall that there are tools and tactics for cutting back on social media use. Turn off notifications that summon you back to social media throughout the day, and set time limits on individual apps. Limit the number of people you follow and the number of platforms on your devices. These new social media habits can help reduce your sense of social media anxiety.

Social media offers limitless diversions, but try to limit your social media use by prioritizing the activities and interactions that you find the most meaningful or enjoyable.

CHAPTER 5

SEEKING HELP

If you're experiencing social media anxiety, there are people who can help you cope with the situation. Chances are, some of your friends also have mixed feelings about social media even if it doesn't cause anxiety issues. Your family and friends will probably support you and help you in your effort to overcome your issues if you tell them about your difficulties with social media anxiety.

A mental health professional can also help you deal with social media anxiety and the problems it causes in your life. Social media can affect people's moods and emotions in complex ways. Therapists recognize that there are both positive and negative aspects to social media, and they can help patients set boundaries and establish control over their social media use.

TURNING TO FAMILY AND FRIENDS

Your friends and family should be the first people you turn to when dealing with something difficult like social media anxiety. They care about you and your well-being, so they are invested in finding solutions to your problems because what affects you affects them. Not only that, but they are also some of the people with whom you spend the most time in your day-to-day life and are well situated to help you change your habits. You can also ask your classmates or coworkers for support.

The more time you spend with people in person, the less time you'll have to spend online, and the less you'll be tempted to go on social media.

One of the best ways for your friends and family to help you cope with social media anxiety is to spend time with you in person. Instead of keeping in touch online, you could share a meal with them or go out and do something together. Not only will this mean you won't have to turn to social media for interactions, but also if they can engage you enough, you won't feel compelled to check what's happening online while you're with them.

Your friends and family can also hold you accountable for your social media use. If you tell them that you're cutting back on your social media use or even quitting completely, they can call you out if they see you commenting on a post or checking your phone while you're with them. This takes some of the pressure off of you, so you don't always have to be self-disciplined and resist temptation. If no one else knows you're trying not to use social media, then it's completely up to you to make sure you're not using it. If your friends and family know, however, then you have some backup just in case you ever slip up.

A good friend should be willing to back you up when trying to cut back on social media time.

TURNING TO A MENTAL HEALTH PROFESSIONAL

The other people who can help with your social media anxiety are the professionals: doctors, counselors, therapists, and psychologists. These people are qualified to deal with the situations you're experiencing. They've seen these problems before, and it's their job to handle them in the most appropriate way.

If social media is the only thing causing you anxiety, then you probably won't need sustained professional help, but checking in with your doctor can't hurt. If social media anxiety is only a part of a bigger problem for you, however, then therapy might be just what you need.

If you have a general practitioner (GP)—your regular doctor—they can assess your symptoms and determine whether you are suffering from a mental health condition. If your GP thinks therapy is a good option, they can refer you to a variety of specialists in your area. A school counselor might also be able to refer you to a therapist. There are also reliable sites online that provide listings for mental health professionals.

If your GP or school counselor refers you to a therapist, they will most likely be practicing a form of cognitive behavioral therapy (CBT). CBT is the most widely used form of therapy for treating mental disorders, including anxiety and depression. The focus of CBT is to change how you think. The theory is that changing your thoughts will change your behaviors, which will in turn change your feelings. For instance, if social media is making you feel anxious because you feel overwhelmed trying to keep up with everything that your friends are posting, you might be thinking, "I need to stay up-to-date with everything on Facebook." Your therapist would then help you to instead think, "It doesn't matter if I miss something on social media occasionally." This would lead you to check social media less often and feel less anxious and overwhelmed by it.

Mental health professionals recognize that social media use can affect mental health, and they can offer strategies for managing negative aspects of social media.

Another type of therapy called exposure therapy is specifically designed to treat anxiety disorders. The name describes its process: exposure therapy exposes patients to the things that cause them distress. The idea is that the more often you are exposed to the object or situation, the more accustomed to it you will become, the more in control you will feel, and the less anxiety you will experience. Exposure therapy uses a technique called systematic desensitization, in which you take small steps to build up your confidence before facing the thing that you're afraid of. For example, if you're anxious about using social media because you have experienced cyberbullying in the past, you might begin by just looking at screenshots from various social media platforms, then imagining using them, then just signing in and looking at other people's pages for a few minutes, and eventually posting something on your own page.

Occupational therapy is another form of therapy that is often used to treat anxiety and is viewed as especially useful for younger patients. The goal of occupational therapy is to help the patient acquire or regain the skills needed for daily life. An occupational therapist might help someone with social media anxiety focus on time management, breathing techniques, healthy sleep patterns, and conversational skills. These skills will help the person be less dependent on social media and deal better with it when using it.

Occupational therapy focuses less on thoughts than on concrete actions people can take to deal with their problems and to prevent problems from occurring in the first place.

In choosing a therapist, look for someone with a background in working with teens who suffer from anxiety disorders or self-esteem issues.

It's important to note that therapists will often use a combination of different forms of therapy in treating a single patient. Each person is unique and will respond differently to different techniques. A therapist's job is to find the most effective way of treating each individual patient, whether that be CBT or a combination of different therapies.

Also remember that therapists aren't one-size-fits-all. Not every therapist works well for everyone. If you're not getting along with your therapist, it's OK to ask to see someone else. Just because it's not working with you and one particular therapist doesn't mean that therapy can't be helpful for you—you probably just haven't found the right person yet.

Social media anxiety can negatively affect many aspects of your daily life. If you're considering how you can address your social media anxiety, you're already making progress. As seen, there are many tools and techniques that can help you change your social media habits. There are also people you can turn to for help. Dealing with the issue will reduce symptoms of social media anxiety—such as low self-esteem, trouble focusing, and insomnia—and make you feel better about yourself.

10 GREAT QUESTIONS TO ASK A PSYCHOLOGIST

1. Do you think social media anxiety should be classified as a clinical condition?

2. How is social media anxiety different from social anxiety disorder?

3. Am I suffering solely from social media anxiety or am I also experiencing other mental disorders?

4. Is medication an effective way to treat social media anxiety?

5. Should I unplug from social media entirely or just cut back on how much I use it?

6. What do you think the best form of therapy would be for my situation?

7. Have you seen an increase in the number of people experiencing social media anxiety?

8. Which social media platforms have you found cause the most anxiety?

9. How is anxiety caused by social media different from anxiety caused by other things?

10. Overall, do you consider social media to be more of a help or a hindrance to people?

A psychologist can help you examine your own habits, behavior, and emotional states regarding social media to understand how it affects your mental well-being.

GLOSSARY

account A social media user's profile, which stores information and allows access to a platform by signing in with a username and password.

anxiety A feeling of worry or stress about a future event.

anxiety disorder A disorder marked by fear or stress beyond the usual reaction to something.

blue light The light given off by screens that signals to the brain that it is time to wake up.

cognitive behavioral therapy (CBT) A form of therapy that focuses on changing people's thoughts and behaviors.

cyberbullying When people use social media and other forms of digital communication to bully others.

deactivate To temporarily close a social media account, thereby making it inaccessible, but saving the information so the account can be reopened.

feed The main page of a social media platform where all the posts by people with whom a user is connected appear.

multitasking Trying to do two or more things at once but actually just switching quickly back and forth between them.

notification A message that pops up on a mobile device, usually sent by an app to inform the user of something that has happened.

platform A social media service, such as Facebook, Twitter, or Instagram.

post When a user shares text, images, audio, video, or anything else from their computer or device on a social media platform.

scrolling Moving up and down through social media feeds to navigate through content that has been posted.

selfie A photo one takes of oneself, usually with a cell phone.

smartphone A mobile phone with functions similar to a computer, with the ability to run apps and access the internet.

social media Websites and apps people use to connect with people, communicate, and share content.

unplugging Removing oneself from social media for an extended period of time.

FOR MORE INFORMATION

ANXIETY AND DEPRESSION ASSOCIATION OF AMERICA (ADAA)

8701 Georgia Avenue, Suite 412
Silver Spring, MD 20910
Email: information@adaa.org
Website: adaa.org
Facebook:
@AnxietyAndDepressionAssociationOfAmerica
Instagram: @triumphoveranxiety
Twitter: @Got_Anxiety
The Anxiety and Depression Association of America (ADAA) is an international nonprofit organization that works toward the prevention, treatment, and cure of disorders such as anxiety and depression through science, treatment, and education.

ANXIETY CANADA

400-601 West Broadway
Vancouver, BC, V5Z 4C2
Canada
(604) 620-0744
Website: www.anxietycanada.com
Facebook: @AnxietyCanada
Instagram and Twitter: @anxiety_canada
Anxiety Canada is a nonprofit organization devoted to raising awareness among Canadians about anxiety and supporting access to resources and treatment.

ANXIETY.ORG

4600 Campus Drive, Suite 107
Newport Beach, CA 92660
(949) 267-4117
Website: www.anxiety.org
Facebook: @AnxietyDotOrg
Twitter: @Anxietyorg
Anxiety.org is dedicated to providing resources to help people with anxiety understand and overcome their condition.

COMMON SENSE MEDIA

San Francisco Headquarters
699 Eighth Street, Suite C150
San Francisco, CA 94103
(415) 863-0600
Website: www.commonsense.org
Facebook: @commonsensemedia
Twitter: @commonsense
Common Sense Media reviews and researches the media and technology used by kids. Common Sense Education (www.commonsense.org/education/) provides educational resources to empower kids to become savvy digital citizens.

CYBERBULLYING RESEARCH CENTER

Website: cyberbullying.org
Facebook, Instagram: @cyberbullyingresearch
Twitter: @onlinebullying
The Cyberbullying Research Center provides information on cyberbullying among adolescents, including resources on the misuse of social media.

THE CYBERSMILE FOUNDATION

530 Lytton Avenue, 2nd Floor
Palo Alto, CA 94301
Email: help@cybersmile.org
Website: www.cybersmile.org
Facebook: @TheCybersmileFoundation
Instagram: @cybersmilefoundation
Twitter: @CybersmileHQ
The Cybersmile Foundation is a nonprofit organization that works to fight online bullying and abuse, and promotes a safe, positive digital community.

PSYCHOLOGY TODAY

115 E. Twenty-Third Street, 9th Floor
New York, NY 10010
Website: www.psychologytoday.com
Facebook: @psychologytoday
Instagram: @psych_today
Twitter: @psychtoday
Psychology Today is a magazine and online site focusing on psychology and mental health. It provides listings for mental health professionals as well as resources on issues such as dealing with anxiety.

TEEN LINE

Cedars-Sinai
PO Box 48750
Los Angeles, CA 90048
(800) 852-8336
Email: admin@teenlineonline.org
Website: www.teenline.org
Facebook, Instagram, and Twitter: @teenlineonline
The Teen Line helpline offers mental health support provided by trained teen counselors.

FOR FURTHER READING

Aman, Jodi. *Anxiety . . . I'm So Done With You: A Teen's Guide to Ditching Toxic Stress and Hardwiring Your Brain for Happiness*. New York, NY: Skyhorse Publishing, 2020.

Bradley, Michael J. *Crazy-Stressed*. New York, NY: AMACOM, 2017.

Cik, Kate Frommer. *Anxiety: The Ultimate Teen Guide*. Lanham, MD: Rowman & Littlefield, 2020.

Harts, Shannon H. *Stress and Anxiety*. Buffalo, NY: Rosen Publishing, 2021.

Hemmen, Lucie. *The Teen Girl's Anxiety Survival Guide: 10 Ways to Conquer Anxiety and Feel Your Best*. Oakland, CA: Instant Help Books, 2021.

Hugstad, Kristi. *Beneath the Surface: A Teen's Guide to Reaching Out When You or Your Friend Is in Crisis*. Novato, CA: New World Library, 2019.

Larson, Paul. *Safe & Sound: Social Media*. Huntington Beach, CA: Teacher Created Materials, 2017.

McKay, C. R. *I Am Being Cyberbullied . . . What's Next?* Buffalo, NY: Rosen Publishing, 2022.

Sales, Nancy Jo. *American Girls: Social Media and the Secret Lives of Teenagers*. New York, NY: Vintage, 2017.

INDEX

P

R

S

T

ABOUT THE AUTHOR

ROBIN BAUSER has written numerous books for children and young adults, including titles addressing current events issues affecting teens. Bauser lives in Chicago.

PHOTO CREDITS

Cover Gelpi/Shutterstock.com; Cover, pp. 1, 3-80 STUDIO DREAM/Shutterstock.com; Cover, p. 1 HIGOOD/Shutterstock.com; pp. 5, 12, 17 Ground Picture/Shutterstock.com; p. 6 Antlii/Shutterstock.com; p. 8 mooremedia /Shutterstock.com; p. 10 aslysun/Shutterstock.com; p. 11 REDPIXEL.PL/Shutterstock.com; p. 13 Vitalii Vodolazskyi/Shutterstock.com; p. 14 LightField Studios/Shutterstock.com; p. 15 kyokyo/Shutterstock.com; p. 21 Rapeepat Pornsipak/Shutterstock.com; p. 23 Kaspars Grinvalds/Shutterstock.com; pp. 25, 41, 64 SeventyFour/Shutterstock.com; p. 27 David Pereiras/Shutterstock.com; p. 30 TheVisualsYouNeed/Shutterstock.com; p. 31 LADO/Shutterstock.com; p. 33 Jacob Lund/Shutterstock.com; p. 35 focal point/Shutterstock.com; p. 37 PanuShot/Shutterstock.com; p. 38 Photo Book Pro/Shutterstock.com; p. 43 Gladskikh Tatiana/Shutterstock.com; p. 45 ORION PRODUCTION/Shutterstock.com; p. 47 asiandelight/Shutterstock.com; p. 49 selinofoto/Shutterstock.com; p. 51 dwphotos/Shutterstock.com; p. 53 Jacek Chabraszewski/Shutterstock.com; p. 55 NINETYONEFOTO/Shutterstock.com; p. 57 Odua Images/Shutterstock.com; p. 59 Dasha Petrenko/Shutterstock.com; p. 61 George Rudy/Shutterstock.com; p. 63 VK Studio/Shutterstock.com; p. 67 Volodymyr TVERDOKHLIB/Shutterstock.com.